BEYOND AN ENTREPRENEUR

Jendayi A. Stafford
Ada Moseley
Frederick and Barbara Bennett
Gail Dickson
Jarrod Stafford
Wanda Curry

Copyright © 2020 by Jendayi A. Stafford

All rights reserved. This book or any portion thereof may not be reproduced or used in any manner whatsoever without the express written permission of the publisher except for the use of brief quotations in a book review.

Printed in the United States of America

First Printing, 2020

ISBN 978-1-64921-309-9

Edited & Formatted by Show Your Success

Published by Jendayi A. Stafford

Table of Contents

Introduction v

Jendayi A. Stafford 1
Ada Moseley 5
Frederick and Barbara Bennett 13
Gail Dickson 23
Jarrod Stafford 33
Wanda Curry 41

Conclusion 55
Featured Author 57

Introduction

Hello aspiring or fellow entrepreneur! Obviously, you have happened upon this book because you are looking to start a business or learn from other entrepreneurs who are successfully running their own.

Starting a business is such an exciting process, but it can become tedious and overwhelming if you let it. So many entrepreneurs lose their fire and passion for their business because of the numerous obstacles they had to face in getting it up and running. They didn't look beyond the product or services. There is so much more to running a business than just your products and services, and these featured entrepreneurs are here to share that information with you!

In this book, you will hear from several successful entrepreneurs who have gone through and overcome several obstacles in getting their businesses up and running. The insights they provide are one of a kind! You will learn valuable lessons to help you through the start-up process and beyond.

These entrepreneurs are from several professions including a salon owner and hair care expert,

Introduction

a general contractor and a holistic whole-body care coach. These entrepreneurs provide their personal experiences of being in business for themselves, as well as lessons and guidelines they have learned. They have collaborated on this project to help generations of entrepreneurs be able to maximize their businesses.

Throughout this book, you will not only learn lessons and guidelines from experienced entrepreneurs who have been successfully building their businesses for more than a combined 50 years, but you will also receive some of the most current facts about entrepreneurship within the United States.

Jendayi A. Stafford

Facebook	https://jendayiastafford.com/
Facebook	https://www.facebook.com/JendayiAStafford/
Instagram	https://www.instagram.com/dcbaby_valady/
Linked-In	https://www.linkedin.com/in/jendayistafford/

I am the owner of Mission Counseling & Consulting, LLC, located in Virginia. We offer a variety of services, from our online school I.N.K. Academy (inspiring you with new knowledge, as well as helping you discover, recover and grow!) to our holistic whole-body care coaching.

Holistic whole-body care coaching is specific only to Mission Counseling & Consulting, LLC. It is a combination of all my training and experience as a marriage and family therapist/mental health counselor, integrative nutrition health coach, pharmacy technician, minister and life coach. I use each and every one of these professional skills to help my clients from a whole-body perspective. As a therapist, I realize that people have mental health issues that may stem from their nutrition or their spiritual life. However, as a therapist, it is outside of my scope of practice to assist any of those areas in depth. As a holistic whole-body care coach, I am able to provide my clients with a more whole-body care approach; physical, mental, spiritual, relationship and social.

As I have gone through my time of entrepreneurship and owning my own business, one of the biggest lessons I have learned along the way is to never be afraid to evolve. In the world of business, you either evolve or repeat! You learn to evolve in your current area of expertise or profession to help meet the needs of your clients, or you repeat the same mistakes and continue to fail within your business.

When developing your business, whether you are starting from scratch or you are already established, understand that you DO NOT have to share your vision with everyone! God gave YOU the vision, because YOU have what it takes to make it a reality, even when you think you don't. Like Gideon in Judges chapter 6, you may find yourself questioning God on whether you are the right one for the job. But just as God replied to Gideon, He will provide you with everything you need in order to succeed in your calling.

Remember, God qualifies those whom He calls! God will put people in your path who have a specific specialty you need in order to get up and running or to expand on what you already have in place. If you share your vision with too many people, they may bring discouragement. Remember, people thought Noah was crazy for building a giant ark when there had been no rain (Gen 1:6-7, Gen 7:11). People won't always understand your vision, especially if it seems impossible or unnecessary, or ridiculous to them. EVERYTHING seems impossible until it has been done! Keep the vision! Write it down and make it plain (Habakkuk 2:2)! Protect your vision! Remember, God has already qualified YOU to carry out the vision He gave YOU!

Ada Moseley

Website	https://creadastyle.com/
Facebook	https://www.facebook.com/Creadastyle/
Instagram	https://www.instagram.com/creada0274/
Linked-In	https://www.linkedin.com/in/ada-moseley-12b681b4/

Ada Moseley

Ada F. Moseley is a wife to Jerome Moseley of 15 years, a mother to three adult children and two adoptive children, as well as a grandmother. She hails from Memphis, Tennessee and now resides on beautiful Whidbey Island. She is a licensed minister and has been a licensed hair restorer for over 28 years. Ada attended The Health Care Training Institute in Memphis, TN, as well as the Mount Vernon Beauty School. It is through her training at these prestigious schools that she learned people skills and gained a compassion for people and their needs.

Ada is the owner and operator of CreAda's Hair & Wig Salon in Oak Harbor, WA. She specializes in providing personalized hair care for all hair types. Ada provides the highest quality of hair care and hair products in the Pacific Northwest. Ada has an extensive educational background with haircutting, natural haircare specialists, and product knowledge.

Ada has a passion for making people feel great about themselves through hair restoration and care. She values diversity and respect and is known for her ability to make every client feel special. Ada can do the unthinkable, without compromising the integrity of your hair & the value of your time.

What is the name of your business?
CreAda Styles Hair & Wig Salon

What services do you provide?
We offer haircuts, color, hair extensions, natural hair care and waxing in a relaxed, friendly atmosphere.

How is your business set up (Sole Proprietor, LLC, S Corp, Non-Profit) and what made you choose that business model?
Sole Proprietor (for now). I am in the process of getting an LLC because I want my business separated from my personal.

Why did you start your own business?
I was a single parent when I started my business. This allowed more flexibility with my schedule. Also, I had a desire to do more in the hair industry. I knew working for someone was not something I wanted to do for the rest of my career.

What have been some of the biggest learning curves/lessons that you have learned while being in business for yourself?

Lots of lessons have been learned in this small business world. Learning never ends. I learned that you can't please everyone, as much as I would have loved too. I tried to service everyone and soon realized it was not possible. And that was ok.

I've also learned to keep good records, separate cash accounts from personal accounts and not be afraid to ask for help. Starting out, I thought I knew everything about running a business. I soon realized I couldn't do it by myself.

What advice/words of wisdom would you give to someone who is trying to start a business?

The advice I would give is first is to consult the Lord. Give Him the opportunity to pour His desires into you. Next, do your research. Learn as much as you can about what you want to do. Talk to other business owners who have succeeded, and those who might have failed in that industry. It's important to hear and get wise counsel advice from others. And last but not least, it has to be a passion. When you do what you love it's less of a job, and more like walking out your dream every day.

How did you go about creating your business plan? For example, how did you get the basic things you needed to operate, figure out what your profits needed to be per month to be able to pay any overhead and still be able to earn a livable income, etc.

The first time I started a business, I didn't have a plan; I just jumped right in with no idea of what to do. Needless to say, that didn't work. I thought that if I just worked hard, everything would work out. I had the desire, but no plans or money. It caused a lot of grief in the end, but I also learned what not to do and what I needed to do the next time around. So I did some research, asked for help and wrote down everything I needed to have and do. Back then money was low, but I began to put everything on paper and create a plan, save what I could and stick to it.

What are the pros of being in business for yourself?

I have the freedom to do what God has put in my heart to do. I can set the atmosphere for my business. There is nothing better than seeing your heart at work in other people's lives. I have flexibility with my schedule and my ideas.

What are the cons of being in business for yourself?

You have no time for laziness. When you work for yourself you can't do things halfway, because it shows. Also, you have to be able to lead all the time. If something goes wrong, there is no time to blame others because it's all you. And last but not least, it may seem like you will never get to your goal, but if you hang in there and stay consistent, you'll see great things start to happen. You'll see the vision coming to life.

What is the quote/scripture/motto that you operate your business by?

Isaiah 55:8-9. "For My thoughts are not your thoughts, neither are your ways My ways," declares the Lord. "For as the heavens are higher than the earth, so My ways are higher than your ways and My thoughts than your thoughts."

My slogan is: Creating lasting results inside and out! And my motto is to give everyone who comes into my shop the best care possible. It's not just a hair thing, it's also about how good you make that person feel when they come and leave your establishment.

Why did you choose to operate your business off of this quote/scripture/motto?

This scripture became my motivation when I started for the second time because I knew it couldn't be my own thoughts and ideas that would make this business successful. It had to be God's thoughts. He has given me ways to keep it going, and ideas that I thought were too much for me to accomplish. He's constantly reminding me that with Him, I can do all things.

Frederick and Barbara Bennett

Website https://shonufffoods.com
Instagram https://www.instagram.com/shonufffoods/

Frederick and Barbara Bennett are both from Brooksville, FL. Fred graduated from the Art Institute of Seattle, WA for Culinary Arts after earning his Culinary Certification from Skagit Valley College in Mount Vernon, WA. Barbara graduated from Skagit Valley College in Mount Vernon, WA with a Culinary Arts degree as well, she also served in the United States Navy. They both had a vision of owning a business from a very young age, prior to meeting each other. They had unique childhood experiences that allowed them both to hide the stresses of life by being in the kitchen. Learning at the hands and feet of their grandmothers, mothers, fathers and big mommas of their neighborhoods. This vision became a reality when Fred realized that working for others was not his passion. Their goal is to bring the foods from both childhood and traveling experiences to their business. Although being an entrepreneur is definitely not easy. However, it does have its rewards. They both get through the daily struggles of being an entrepreneur by remembering what they went through as children. The struggles from the past helps them get through the future. The biggest reminder in this world is "God first, family second".

What is the name of your business?
ShoNuff Foods, LLC

What services do you provide?
We provide catering, lunch services and a little bit of everything with far as food service industry.

How is your business set up (Sole Proprietor, LLC, S Corp, Non-Profit) and what made you choose that business model?
It is an LLC. We originally started off as a sole proprietor and then as we grew, we decided to change it to an LLC. The LLC helps us with separating the business from the personal. So it's a way to tidy up our business doings just in case something happens.

Why did you start your own business?
We just wanted to provide food that we were missing from back home. Also with just working out here, working for other people, especially for the wages I was earning at the time, I was better off starting a company for myself to provide for my family.

And also, it was something we had talked about from when we were teenagers, you know, back in high school. It was kind of one of the things that we really wanted to do, and then it just came to that point when we moved up here to the West Coast that the opportunity came around and we decided to go for it.

What have been some of the biggest learning curves/lessons that you have learned while being in business for yourself?

The biggest learning curve for me was how to do business and then with doing business, you learn. There isn't one true step-by-step book on how to run a business. There are so many avenues in business operations, but I would say the biggest learning curve is just my day-to-day, whether it's invoicing, finances or customer service and dealing with people. It has been a huge learning curve because everybody is different. Each client has different needs. Each person is different, so it's just learning how to deal with the different characteristics of whoever comes into your establishment.

The other thing for me and my biggest lesson was that I had to learn my value, because if I hadn't learned how to put a value on myself, somebody else would put a value on me. I had to learn how to develop my backbone and learn how to stand real quick.

Another lesson I've learned is accepting my product as intended, because it's really easy to present it one way and have someone come along to try to get my to switch my goal for how I want my product to be presented. So it's holding firm of who you are from beginning to end in promoting your products.

What advice/words of wisdom would you give to someone who is trying to start a business?

Go in flexible because very often in markets, although you might go with targeting one thing, the market dictates to you what it is really looking for. You need to be flexible enough to pivot when the market is telling you to. The big thing is to make sure that you don't put borders upon yourself because whether it be one state or another, or another city, you have the right to make a living and to do it to the best of your ability. And you can't let something as simple as gas hinder you. You must be able to gas up and go where you need to go to perform your business efficiently.

How did you go about creating your business plan? For example, how did you get the basic things you needed to operate, figure out what your profits needed to be per month to be able to pay any overhead and still be able to earn a livable income, etc.

I was in the restaurant business for 17 years before we started this business. I had the privilege of opening up a lot of new restaurants and working under a lot of chefs, so I've done the cost control and the ordering. The restaurant business is the law of thirds. It's very generic, but if you can imagine a pie, slice it up into thirds. So 1/3 would be your bill, another third is your cost of goods sold and the last third is profits. So the way you divide that up is up to each individual or facility; everybody has their own formula. Some restaurants prefer the food cost to be in the 35%, 40% or 50% range. Typically, food costs need to be within 25% to 30% in order to make your slice of the pie worth it at the end of the day.

What are the pros of being in business for yourself?

The biggest thing is that a lot of people have the notion that you set your own time, your own hours and all that. That's actually a lie because you need to be flexible enough to cater to the market you're in because the market isn't necessarily going to cater to you. The biggest advantage I think we have is just that. We're not rooted and grounded into a specific philosophy other than to produce the best food at the highest quality to the best of our ability and that's the only thing we're really rooted in. Right now, the market is telling us to close earlier because they view us as a lunch place. But that flexibility is the biggest advantage we have. We don't have to worry about getting corporate approval to do X, Y and Z because we aren't corporate.

We definitely have a bit more freedom to do certain things than we would if we were working for somebody else. You have the freedom to be creative in your own business. When you're working for somebody else, you may not be able to have that flexibility in your creativity.

What are the cons of being in business for yourself?

Taxes and bills.

And on top of that too, I think another con would be that you don't always get to have time for yourself. You have to be purposeful and set aside time because no matter what you do, it's your business and your downtime. You have staff and give your staff time off, and your time off will easily end up being whatever paperwork you can get to earlier in the week or those meetings you didn't get a chance to attend. You're it. So if you're not ready for that, it can be a very hard thing to deal with as a business owner if you don't realize that your time, you're it.

Another thing is that when somebody has something negative to say about you, when you work for somebody else you can be like, "They're just talking about the restaurant." You can kind of swallow it better. But when it is just you and they're talking trash about you, you kind of take that more to heart and it weighs on you when you actually care about what you're doing. When you put your heart on the plate essentially like we do, every negative comment holds a little bit of weight. So you have to learn how to decompress and put things emotionally where they need to be.

You see it all. You see the good, the bad and the ugly. As a business owner, you should know that you will see the good, the bad and the ugly. You see it all from all angles and from everybody.

What is the quote/scripture/motto that you operate your business by?

Honestly, we don't have something like that, but I will also say this: The very credence of why we're here as Christians is to be a shining example to lead people to Christ. In general, the reason why we have this business, we've always did the business from day one not necessarily as just a way to make money but for a way to care for others. We've been very fortunate for all the duds we've had for employees and things like that. We also had some people do some major turn-around in their lives and for every tear, every drop of blood, every trip to the hospital we've had to take, it's worth it when somebody changed their life around and you are able to see it. So from that model, just pure hard work and the joy of seeing other people's lives transform just from cooking is a beautiful thing.

Why did you choose to operate your business off of this quote/scripture/motto?

Even though we may not have a set quote or scripture things like that to go off of, we just hold true to our Christian values. We really try to live our lives the way God would want us to. And our business is also part of our life. And so although you'll see more of a business side from us, we are who we are through and through. We don't have to hide anything. We care about everybody who walks through our doors, from customer to staff members to somebody who is just dropping by. So we just really try to live our lives in the way God would want us to.

It's not so much of why we choose to because once you accept the call, you know to turn your life around and walk with the Lord. It's not necessarily why you choose. It should be a question of why you're being chosen to do such. And I feel very privileged to be chosen although it's a tiring role. And you don't realize it's tiring until you stop moving, but the privilege is still there and I do thank the Lord for the privilege He has given us.

Gail Dickson

Facebook   https://www.facebook.com/small blessin

Gail Roebuck-Dickson is a native of Connecticut. She grew up and graduated from Westhill High of 76. She started volunteering at her Local Radio Station to support her Community Center in Stamford Conn; WSTC Radio. Gail furthered her education at Grahm Jr College, where she received her FCC License in Boston, Mass., with additional focus not only Radio Communications but Television as well.

Gail moved to Northern Virginia and lived there for over 20 years. While living in Virginia, family health issues made Gail decided to further her education in Healthcare and she went back to school to receive her CNA License and Associate of Science and Medical Assisting Certificate.

Gail made another move to Houston Texas once her children had moved on to pursue their dreams. This move was where she found the real purpose and vision for the development of Small Blessin, non-profit. Her story just goes to show you that there is no age or time limit to finding your passion and purpose.

Gail is the mother of 3 Adults children, 2 beautiful women and 1 handsome man and five grandchildren.

What is the name of your business?
Small Blessin

What services do you provide?
Non-food care packages. The packages are for single females or males and fixed-income families anywhere in the United States.

How is your business set up (Sole Proprietor, LLC, S Corp, Non-Profit) and what made you choose that business model?
The services I provide are a non-profit organization. I made this non-profit because it's a unique service that doesn't provide a personal name on the packages; we send the packages to families with just Small Blessin to show there is someone watching over them.

Why did you start your own business?
I found that being a single mom, you could always find food whenever needed for your family but never could find anything in the sense of necessities for the household. You know, like body soap, detergent for clothing, toothpaste, mouthwash and many other necessities we use daily.

What have been some of the biggest learning curves/lessons that you have learned while being in business for yourself?

In the beginning, I would say it's a support system. Now I would say finding families. I know there are families out there, but I'm having a hard time finding families that are in need. My very first endeavor was sending packages to non-active veterans in the state of Washington on behalf of another non-profit, Veterans Transition Support & Development Center in Oak Harbor. The center also introduced Small Blessin in their local paper in Oak Harbor. When I started, I also supplied care bags to single woman in local shelters in Houston, Texas. I have been providing care packages in Connecticut, Georgia, Virginia and many other places. I am now providing packages to churches and missionary ministries that provide help in their community. I felt this would be another way of spreading love to other families that may not attend church.

What advice/words of wisdom would you give to someone who is trying to start a business?

Keep your vision alive, no matter how long it takes you to achieve what you want to do. Keep yourself focused at all costs, making sure that it's your passion because if it's not your passion, you'll get to a point where you'll be very disappointed in things that are not getting done ASAP. And sometimes you want things to happen right away. They don't. I have also found that sometimes people tend to say they like what you are doing but don't give you the resources or their time. But if you have the patience, God will guide you toward achieving your goal and direct you to meet the proper people, and from there, you will have unlimited success.

How did you go about creating your business plan? For example, how did you get the basic things you needed to operate, figure out what your profits needed to be per month to be able to pay any overhead and still be able to earn a livable income, etc.

Considering that my non-profit is a care package service, I always sit down and access the needs of each family given to me or even ones that I feel may need an extra hand or a personal touch. Being a single mom for a long time, I realized that every family's needs are different. So it's been really easy for me to understand what a single mom or a single dad might need in a household. As a fixed-income family, you always need to balance your money, and think if food is more important or if you need to get what is necessary for the house, then realizing you have bills to pay or your utilities may get cut off. That's not something some families might worry about but when you're a single parent or on a fixed income, it's important to keep yourself balanced.

Since this is a non-profit, I pretty much used part of the 10% intended for my tithes to purchase the items I feel are needed for a family. I try to keep an inventory of body soaps, detergents and stuff like that, just to be prepared to provide a package to a family. One time, I did a care package for a child who had cancer, so I pretty much thought of all items that would make him smile and gave him necessities that his parents would have to purchase themselves to take care of some of their burdens.

What are the pros of being in business for yourself?

I can work anytime I want. That's not a good answer: Everybody says that, and it's a good point, but it can give you time to do some volunteering with agencies. But I think it's the point of being able to provide time for your passion. My passion is to always help people. And so it gives me the extra time to be able to expand my love and joy of helping people.

What are the cons of being in business for yourself?

You can get off track. It's easy sometimes to get tossed around just under the hustle of everyday life. Like I mentioned before, you have to stay focused. Sometimes it's hard to get back on track. It's really important to remember why you wanted to do what you do. It's important to know why you should keep going and know that it's not just helping others but also helping them to feel they can keep the faith to keep going forward in life. I keep a little note in my purse to remind myself that it's something important that I have highlighted in my life anywhere I go. If I go to the dollar store and see someone with one or two items, I will pay for them and tell them to forward to someone else. It's that simple. One time, I was even in the post office and a gentleman was behind me he wanted one stamp. I didn't have one so when it was my turn, I told the man to come up with me and I paid for the stamp. He was so shocked and thankful. It's just letting people know that someone cares, and that we are in this world together to make it together.

What is the quote/scripture/motto that you operate your business by?

A motto is, "Always remember to be a blessing to someone." That came about with me wanting to show people that it doesn't take a lot of money to help someone when you see the need. My scripture, may be long but it's important to understand what God would want us to do. It's Luke 6:38. "Give to others and God will give unto you. Indeed, you will receive a full measure, a generous helping poured into your hand - all that you can hold. The measure that you use for others is the one that God will use for you."

Why did you choose to operate your business off of this quote/scripture/motto?

We need to show our love in the world. When I do each package, it is done anonymously because God does things for everybody in the sense of a miracle. In my opinion, these packages are a miracle just to be able to open the boxes and not have to feel it's another bill. I want someone to open a package and say, "Oh, wow. Someone was thinking of me only me." The package is to help people to keep the *Faith* in themselves and to *Believe* that there is always an angel watching over them no matter what they are going through.

Jarrod Stafford

Website https://themguysconstruction.com
Facebook https://www.facebook.com/themguysconstruction
Instagram https://www.instagram.com/jarrod.stafford.52/

Jarrod Stafford is a married, father of three from Tipp City, Ohio. He has over 12 years of experience in the field of construction. Jarrod has always worked for someone else's company doing everything from excavation and roofing to cleaning up the construction site. It wasn't until a "fluke" conversation occurred that he began his business almost 4 years ago.

Jarrod is the owner and founder of ThemGuys. His company focuses primarily on remodels and handyman type work. During ThemGuys' years of operation, they have completed over 100 remodels and other services including lawn care, handyman repairs, decks, sheds, and home additions.

As the owner of his own company, Jarrod understands the highs and lows that come with being an entrepreneur. He understands the learning curve that must take place in order for growth to occur. It is his desire to teach others how to use the world of construction to build and create, all while being able to maintain their own business.

What is the name of your business?
The name of my business is ThemGuys Construction.

What services do you provide?
I provide light construction. Anywhere from general maintenance to remodels and additions.

How is your business set up (Sole Proprietor, LLC, S Corp, Non-Profit) and what made you choose that business model?
My business is currently a sole proprietor, but with all intentions of changing the format to an LLC.

Why did you start your own business?
I started my own business actually as a fluke. A family friend, Mya, had asked me to take care of their yard while they were on deployment, and so I did that. During that time, I realized I enjoyed working for myself. After starting on that one job, Mya kind of talked me into starting my own business because she knew there were other people that needed it, and the business just started from there.

What have been some of the biggest learning curves/lessons that you have learned while being in business for yourself?

The biggest lesson that I've learned so far is to not be a sole proprietor. If you have the ability, start off with an LLC. There's not a lot of difference in the cost, but the business format is much better, financially and tax-wise. And one of the other lessons I learned is to pay your taxes on time because you don't want them to creep up on you later. The IRS is not to be messed with.

What advice/words of wisdom would you give to someone who is trying to start a business?

My biggest advice would be, just believe in yourself. Don't listen to other people and just do it. Starting a business, depending on what type it is, isn't a very hard thing as long as you believe and trust in yourself and don't listen to people who are going to drag you down. You'll never know what you can achieve until you allow yourself to try.

How did you go about creating your business plan? For example, how did you get the basic things you needed to operate, figure out what your profits needed to be per month to be able to pay any overhead and still be able to earn a livable income, etc?

In my line of work, it's been rather simple. I've always been in and around construction. So having at least a limited amount of tools necessary to start off was rather simple. You don't need a lot of tools, trucks and all these things to really start working in the construction field. I also started out working by myself so I didn't really have any overhead. For the most part, I bought tools that I needed along the way, rented what I couldn't afford and from there, all my work was pretty much profit.

As far as the scheduling and paperwork/administration part goes, my wife took care of the initial set up and then helped me get it to where I could handle it myself.

What are the pros of being in business for yourself?

You can't beat being your own boss! You know, setting your own hours, taking a vacation when you want. I'd say those are some great pros of being self-employed. Also being able to spend time with the family when necessary, and taking emergency leave that you don't have to ask for.

What are the cons of being in business for yourself?

Sometimes if you don't have the hustle or the motivation, it can be hard to get consistent business. For me specifically, I work a job that can tend to be seasonal so that makes it rough come wintertime. And then depending on where you're at, it can be hard to find the right help when you need it when you start hiring and working on bigger jobs that you can't do alone.

What is the quote/scripture/motto that you operate your business by?

My motto is: Customers first, money second, quality always.

Why did you choose to operate your business off of this quote/scripture/motto?

I believe that if you're in it to help people and if you really like your job or love your job, then to satisfy a customer is the most fulfilling part of the job. My grandpa always told me that if your job is your hobby, you'll never work a day in your life. And so if you're chasing money, you're always going to be chasing money. And if you're always chasing money, you'll never truly be satisfied with what you're doing.

Wanda Curry

Website	AuthorWandaCurry.com
Facebook	https://www.facebook.com/wanda.curryshepardt
Linked-In	https://www.linkedin.com/in/wanda-curry-shepard-4b918794/

Wanda D. Curry has always enjoyed teaching others. Her first assignment dates back to 1985 during the 7th grade, when she was selected by her teacher to assist in teaching

English to a peer, who moved to Columbus, OH from Honduras.

Ms. Wanda was trained in leadership and business by her Bishop and Entrepreneurial Mentor, Dr. Christine C. McGee. She learned that you must have a holistic approach, which addresses emotional, physical, and Spiritual barriers when instructing individuals. Under Bishop McGee, Wanda obtained a Ministerial License of Deaconess, Diploma of Practical Theology from the International Seminary, and Instructor's license from the Evangelical Training Association. She also took courses in Bible Survey, Survival Kit, Living Your Christian Values and Ecclesiology.

She currently holds the Professional Designation of Certified Fraud Examiner (CFE); a Bachelor's of Science in Accounting with a minor in Healthcare Management degree from Franklin University; Associates of Science in Accounting Degree and Bookkeeping Certificate from Columbus State Community College. She is a Licensed Insurance agent in Property, Casualty, Life, Health, and Surety bail bonds for the State of Ohio. She holds other certifications, including certified grant writer.

In her professional career, Ms. Wanda has trained individuals in Entrepreneurial, Professional and Technical positions. In 2009, Ms. Wanda expanded into the transportation industry by opening a brokerage firm. She has trained and employed several agents to arrange the transportation of goods throughout the United States by connecting shippers and carriers. The Logistics division began in 2010 when she began purchasing semi-trucks to transport goods directly for shippers. Recognizing the need for Logistics-related career training, Ms. Wanda began training individuals in dispatching, brokerage, and office management. She developed a curriculum that not only would teach the textbook version of careers but also give the application approach of instruction through an internship at her company.

Ms. Wanda now offers these courses to the general public through Unique Services Logistics Career Academy, LLC. It is her hope that through the training and certifications offered in this academy, people will develop career paths that will lead to self-sufficient, sustaining and successful careers.

What is the name of your business?
Unique Services Logistics

What services do you provide?
We provide three types of services: Freight transportation, passenger transportation and workforce development training.

How is your business set up (Sole Proprietor, LLC, S Corp, Non-Profit) and what made you choose that business model?
We started as an LLC, which was a single-member LLC with myself being the owner. Several years later we changed it to an S Corp, which is a small business designation for a corporation. We started with the single-member LLC because I wanted to have the option of bringing other people to work with me and not have all the liabilities as a sole proprietor.

Why did you start your own business?
I started my own business because I wanted to provide a solution to transportation services and I wanted to be able to have some sustaining income as

an entrepreneur. I wanted to have time and economic freedom.

What have been some of the biggest learning curves/lessons that you have learned while being in business for yourself?

One of the major learning curves I have had to deal with are the highs and lows in business. I have to wear multiple hats as a business owner. Trust me, it's not for the faint of heart. As an entrepreneur, you have to work very hard to obtain a contract, only to be outbid by someone else. You have to have a contingency plan as well as the tenacity to not give up as an entrepreneur.

What advice/words of wisdom would you give to someone who is trying to start a business?

Number one, I would say planning is key, taking time to plan out what you want to do, writing it out and revisiting it that plan often.

Number two, be open to innovation because as an entrepreneur, you should be looking to solve a problem. There are all kinds of problems and things that can be solved that are customer-focused. So don't say, "Well, I started to make book covers, and I will only stick with that." The way our society is and the way things grow and change, you may have to make book covers you can sell online. So you can't say, "Oh, I don't want to sell them online because I just want to make them and take them to a trade store." So always be open to innovation and change.

How did you go about creating your business plan? For example, how did you get the basic things you needed to operate, figure out what your profits needed to be per month to be able to pay any overhead and still be able to earn a livable income, etc?

I started my business plan with just writing, no format, just writing out what I wanted to do. Actually, after I did freehand writing, I felt the purpose that the Lord was giving me for my business, then I went back and wrote down the instructions He gave me. Then I asked how to do it. I began to research the market segments and what would make me unique in the marketplace. I also evaluated how much it was going to cost to operate the business and what my breakeven point was.

Last, I determined how much revenue I would need to generate to become completely self-employed. So, I started working my business part-time as most people do, while I was working another job. For the next two years, I was planning, getting certifications, taking classes that helped me understand what's needed in business. I took money that I earned and used it to buy different things – business cards, a laptop, etc. As far as budgeting and the accounting practice, that is the backbone of any business. So for me, being an accountant was a blessing for me because I'm always focused on the costs associated with any line item in a business. Being able to say, "This is what I need to replace my income once I go full-time in my business," having that written out and then weighing out the difference of having a limited income of $20 an hour as opposed to unlimited income. Being open to unlimited income and having God's favor over my life has allowed me to land several contracts where I could make my back-then annual salary of about $15,000 in one month's time. So just being open to knowing what you want to do, being passionate about it and then having a plan of execution are the top components to starting and growing a business. Also, once you have experienced the highs and lows, you tend to become disciplined enough to know that even though you have money sitting in the bank, you won't be so eager to spend it. You have to manage your money very well to make it stretch.

What are the pros of being in business for yourself?

One of the pros for me is that I love helping people and I'm able to provide a service that is rewarding to me. I consider my business a marketplace ministry. It's a way to meet people. It's a way to train and develop the gifts people have once they come to our training program. If we are transporting passengers, it's a way to take care of people who may be sick or disabled or need a ride to a doctor's appointment. And if it's freight, it's delivering a product for a customer or a company who is depending on us to get their product from point A to point B.

What are the cons of being in business for yourself?

The con is you if you are not a good planner. If you don't have revenue, it can be very stressful. You can want to give up because of the unknown. It truly is a faith walk. So if you're not strong in faith or in the plan that you put in place, it's easy for you to want to give up because you to feel defeated. So you have to tell yourself that there is no failure, there is no quitting! We have to figure it out. So the con would be, it could be mentally straining.

What is the quote/scripture/motto that you operate your business by?

So our company motto is, "We train, We staff, We transport." Because logistics is a worldwide business that touches every industry, I live by the prayer of Jabez where I ask the Lord to enlarge my territory, knowing that He will be the provider. And as He enlarges, He gives us the people to work with us hand in hand to fulfill what we're doing.

Why did you choose to operate your business off of this quote/scripture/motto?

Because of the prayer of Jabez, of enlarging the territory, I believe that you just live by faith. And I believe that God gives all of His children a strategic gift that we are to give to build His Kingdom. And it's not always traditional. So the enlarging of the territory, it's confidence that if He chose you to complete something that may be out of your comfort zone, He's going to be the provider and that the ultimate glory will come to Him.

2019 Entrepreneur Facts

If you have not realized it by now, you are not alone in your entrepreneurial journey! While you are learning from some of our amazing entrepreneurs, here are some fun facts about entrepreneurship!

- 62% of the billionaires in the United States are self-made!
- In 2016, more than 25 million Americans were starting or running their own small business.
- 67% of entrepreneurs use their personal funds to deal with various financial business challenges.
- 15 million Americans are full-time self-employed, and that number is predicted to grow to 27 million by the end of 2020! Will you be one of those 27 million???
- There are more than 582 million entrepreneurs worldwide.
- 33% of entrepreneurs only have a high school diploma.
- The highest number of self-employed professionals (19.6%) work in construction/trade fields.

- Business and food are two of the most popular industries for entrepreneurship.
- 83.1% of U.S. business owners started their company as an entrepreneurial small business.
- The #1 reason businesses fail is because there is no market need for their services or products.
- 62% of small businesses have no staff outside of the business owner.
- 54% of entrepreneurs say they make more money now than when they worked for someone else.
- 97% of entrepreneurs say they would never go back to traditional employment.

(https://www.smallbizgenius.net/by-the-numbers/entrepreneur-statistics/)

Mission Counseling & Consulting, LLC Mentorship Programs

In March 2020, Mission Counseling & Consulting, LLC will launch their mentorship programs. The following programs will be available:

Mission Counseling & Consulting, LLC Young CEO Mentorship Program:
-This program is a mentorship that is focused on teaching our youth the ins and outs of creating and building their own business, from filing the proper paperwork needed to open and operate, to producing a vision statement and goal, to developing a Lean Start-Up Business Plan. The youth will also learn how to properly plan, organize and prioritize daily, weekly, monthly and annual goals. The end result of this mentorship program is for our youth to be able to have a viable and sustainable legitimate business of their own; fully functional and operational. Each child will be matched with a mentor who is a good fit for them in business and personality.

Mission Counseling & Consulting, LLC Young Author Program:

-This program is geared toward helping our youth learn the ins and outs of writing and publishing their own written work. Each young person who goes through this program will have the opportunity to learn step-by-step how to plan, outline, write and publish their very own book. These youths will learn from various authors who have self-published and who have published through a publishing company. They will get to have one-on-one planning sessions with the authors as they write their book. The authors vary in genre from children's books and mental health, to fiction and business.

For more information on these programs, please email info@jendayiastafford.com.

Conclusion

Thank you so much for reading this book! It is my sincere hope that after finishing, you will walk away with more entrepreneurial knowledge than you had before. I hope that you feel more empowered, as though you can overcome some of the obstacles that you may currently face, or may face in the future.

Now, I want you to take a moment to write down three things that stood out to you the most about being an entrepreneur:

1. _____
_____
_____

2. _____
_____
_____

3. _____
_____

Now, I want you to write down three things you learned from the entrepreneurs in this book that you will apply to your own business practices:

Conclusion

1. _____

_____

_____

2. _____

_____

_____

3. _____

_____

_____

    I am so excited for you and your entrepreneurial journey! Feel free to connect with any of us if you have any specific questions about a particular trade or industry that was featured. We look forward to being part of the 27 million entrepreneurs with you!

Featured Author

What is the name of your business?
Art by Heather Lynne

What are the services/products your business provides?
Custom hand lettering and calligraphy for your home and business

What is your business website?
www.artbyheatherlynne.com

What are your business social media handles?

Instagram- @artbyheatherlynne
Facebook- Art by Heather Lynne

What is the most fulfilling part of being an entrepreneur?

I get to decide exactly what I want my business to be. I can do what I love and I can always shift my services to match my own goals and needs.

What guidelines can you share with someone trying to start up a business?

Surround yourself with both peers and mentors that can cheer you on and give you insights. Invest what you can in learning more about your craft and about running a business. Create services or products that are relatable and solve problems. Most importantly, being an entrepreneur takes passion so your business should reflect the things that you are passionate about.

How has being an entrepreneur helped you in your personal life?

It's given me more confidence in myself and in my abilities as an artist.

What is the name of your business?
Designs By Amaya, LLC

What are the services/products your business provides?
- All-natural lip glosses
- Handmade Jewelry
- Logo Designs
- Book Cover Designs

What is your business website?
https://designsbyamaya.com/

What are your business social media handles?
INSTAGRAM: DesignsByAmaya

As a child, what is the most fulfilling part about being an entrepreneur?
I don't have to be 16 to work, the money, and that I get work experience prior to having to enter the workforce.

Why is gaining work experience important to you?
If I ever want to go into the workforce, I can show that I already have the work experience through owning my own business.

What advice would you give one of your friends who was an aspiring entrepreneur?
Just do it! Don't be afraid to put yourself and your product out there.

How has being a young entrepreneur helped you in your life?

It allows me to earn money for things that I want without having to ask my parents for the money.

What are some of the things that you would like to get to help expand your business?

I want to be able to get a circuit, a t-shirt press and a camera so that I can expand my business and earn an additional stream of income.

What are some of the goals that you are hoping for in your business by the time you turn 18?

I want to be able save $5,000

What is the name of your business?
Dutchess, LLC

What are the services/products your business provides?
- All-natural lip balm
- All-natural bath bombs
- All-natural lip scrub

What is your business website?
https://dutchessbyheiress.com/

What are your business social media handles?
FACEBOOK: Dutchessbyheiress

As a child, what is the most enjoyable part about being an entrepreneur?
I enjoy being able to make my products.

What advice would you give one of your friends who was an aspiring entrepreneur?
Just do it! Don't be afraid to put yourself and your product out there.

How has being a young entrepreneur helped you in your life?
It has helped me with being able to make my own money and having the patience to follow directions so that I can finish what I need to do.

What are some of the things that you would like to get to help expand your business?
I want to be able to add lip gloss to my business, because I love using it for myself. I also want to start making my own body lotion one day. I also want to start a hair care line, because I love doing hair.

What are some of the goals that you are hoping for in your business by the time you turn 18?

I want to be able to save at least $3,000, and to have my products featured in major stores like Sephora, Ulta and the Navy Exchange (NEX) stores.

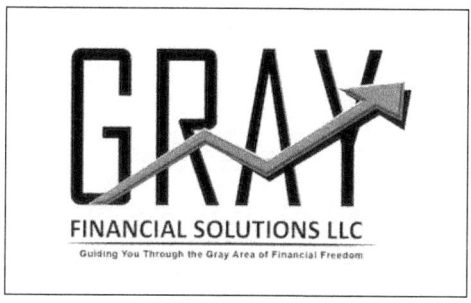

What is the name of your business?
Gray Financial Solutions

What are the services/products your business provides?
- Credit Repair / Credit Building
- Business Credit
- Taxes
- Business Consulting
- Life Insurance
- Debt Consolidation
- Financial Planning

What is your business website?
www.gray-financial.com

What are your business social media handles?
FACEBOOK: Gray Financial Solutions
INSTAGRAM: GrayFinancialSolutions

What is the most fulfilling part of being an entrepreneur?
FREEDOM. Being able to be in full control of your day is such a liberating feeling. You find time to do all the things you need to do, plus a lot of the things you want to without putting it off. Furthermore, you are generating generational wealth for you and your family. Wages are what is used to get you to abandon your dreams. Jim Rohn said it perfectly, "Wages will make you a living while profits will make you a fortune."

What guidelines can you share with someone trying to start up a business?

1. **START.** Too many businesses fail because they simply never start. Stop asking yourself "why you" and start asking "why not you."

2. **Be obsessed with learning.** Never stop the quest of learning more information. Read

books, listen to the greats before and dedicate time to overall self-improvement.

3. **Be clear on what your vision is.** Once you come to terms of what this vision looks like do not let people deter you from that vision. Be willing to stand on that vision even if you are standing alone. It is your duty to sell that vision and get people to buy into it.

How has being an entrepreneur helped you in your personal life?

Becoming an entrepreneur has decreased the stress in our life TREMENDOUSLY. We find ourselves happier, more level headed and intentional in all we do. We are actively creating a life that gives us the means AND THE TIME to whatever it is we want. Life is too short to live for anyone else but yourself and once you have gotten a piece of "the life" you will never look back.

What is the name of your business?
My business name is Heiress Farm, LLC, but we go by Heiress

What are the services/products your business provides?
All-natural skin moisturizer made with simple ingredients from nature that are good for the skin.

What is your business website?
JaniceParkerOhara.com

What is the most fulfilling part of being an entrepreneur?
The flexibility working when I went to working, when I need to be working under my own terms and not answering some notice.

What guidelines can you share with someone trying to start up a business?
Be willing to work as hard for yourself as you did when you were working for somebody else. Also it's an investment of your time and money, so know that you are probably not going to get large financial gains right away.

How has being an entrepreneur helped you in your personal life?
It's boosted my confidence. Since my husband past-- he was really wind beneath my wings. Being in business for myself is really helping me stand on my own two feet again without questioning or relying on him. So, it improved my confidence some, and now I am more willing to put myself out there.

What is the name of your business?
My business name is Heiress Farm, LLC, but we go by Heiress

What are the services/products your business provides?
All-natural skin moisturizer made with simple ingredients from nature that are good for the skin.

What is your business website?
JaniceParkerOhara.com

What is the most fulfilling part of being an entrepreneur?

The flexibility working when I went to working, when I need to be working under my own terms and not answering some notice.

What guidelines can you share with someone trying to start up a business?

Be willing to work as hard for yourself as you did when you were working for somebody else. Also it's an investment of your time and money, so know that you are probably not going to get large financial gains right away.

How has being an entrepreneur helped you in your personal life?

It's boosted my confidence. Since my husband past-- he was really wind beneath my wings. Being in business for myself is really helping me stand on my own two feet again without questioning or relying on him. So, it improved my confidence some, and now I am more willing to put myself out there.

What is the name of your business?
Right Array, LLC

What are the services/products your business provides?
- Entity Formations (Nationwide)
- Minority Certification Preparation & Coaching
- Government Contracting Preparation & Coaching
- Grant Research/Writing
- 501c3 Preparation and 6. TRUE Business Credit Development.

What is your business website?
www.rightarrayllc.com

*What are your business social media handles?
IG is @rightarray
FB is @rightarrayllc
YouTube Channel is https://www.youtube.com/channel/UCV1mGWTPCm8tj2YXNFlYDUQ

What is the most fulfilling part of being an entrepreneur?
Living my life on my own terms with the freedom, flexibility & pay I deserve.

What guidelines can you share with someone trying to start up a business?

1. Never accept failure (if you can fall off a horse and get right back on then you are well suited to be an entrepreneur)
2. Be passionate about your business ownership endeavor and maintain discipline
3. Attitude & consistency are KEY to your success

4. Write down your plan, write down your goals and reach them.

How has being an entrepreneur helped you in your personal life?

1. I celebrate everything especially the small wins; entrepreneurship taught me years ago that even the littlest achievement is a slam-dunk

2. It's not all about me and my businesses; so I lose myself in the service of others, I collaborate & continually make time for family & friends.

What is the name of your business?
SIMPLY BEING MEE, LLC

What are the services/products your business provides?
startup and development coaching, specializing in branding and product photography, resume writing, and lifestyle

What is your business website?
simplybmee.com

What are your business social media handles?
IG- @simplybmee
FB- @simplybmee

What is the most fulfilling part of being an entrepreneur? What guidelines can you share with someone trying to start up a business? How has being an entrepreneur helped you in your personal life?

If you're like me, you may have started with a dream or a series of them. As I'm writing this, the first thing that popped in mind was the infamous question, "What do you want to be when you grow up?" Sounds familiar? Was it volunteering at an animal sanctuary? Being an astronaut and traveling to the moon? Opening a business and being your very own boss?

As a child, my imagination was colossal and immeasurable—a fierce tiger, a hunting lioness, a howling wolf in the middle of the night. I was unstoppable. I was fearless. The stories I read about, heard of and saw in the media bestowed me with inspiration, purpose and aspirations, to dream bigger and strive for better. My soul was on fire. My eyes widened. I could not stop wondering about the things I'll be able to accomplish one day. I had dreams. I had goals. I had passion!

Childhood was as innocent as just that. The older I became, the quicker the flame began to die. I had people tell me to be more realistic, to just go to school and get a stable career with benefits, to stop wasting myself away, because I'm "only getting older," to settle down and have kids and stop dreaming the unthinkable. I hardened up, aimlessly navigated through school and continued working and slaving away with no real ambitions. I was robotic and just existing.

Society, along with many people I met and knew, including myself, tried to put me into a box, a one size fits all glove. And, quite frankly, I'm just not about that life. As someone I trusted once handed it to me, "You're a trailblazer! That's what you are and have been! You've been paving the way for your younger siblings, your culture and yourself." The lightbulb went on, and I started to snap out of the funk. The more those forces tried to mold me the more I resisted.

Something unexpected and overwhelmingly beautiful happened. In my early twenties, I started catching myself dreaming again. Occasionally, that childlike part of me awakened from the long, cold winter nights. I became a bear, full of hunger, who would go out for food, stuff my face, to only return to hibernation. It was a slow, repetitive, but progressive process. The more this phenomenon occurred, the more whole I emerged. My heart started to ache, and my soul started to wander. I began to want more and refused to settle.

To be able to dream is a magical privilege. I believe "entrepreneur" should be the Gemini half to "dreamer." We dream just like everybody else; we need to. However, we are that and more; we are the doers, the risk takers, the transformers, the students, the leaders and the chargers. Having a dream come alive was priceless, an indescribable feeling and sense of achievement like no other. I was Dr. Frankenstein who finally witnessed his creature come to life. It's A-L-I-V-E! Honestly, I probably look like him too from all those sleepless nights—erratic and completely insane, but full of excitement.

Therefore, if I must sum up what was the most fulfilling part of being an entrepreneur, it's just the simple fact of knowing, "I did it!" Even if I'm not always active with my business and not quite sure where I am heading, I love meeting like-minded individuals and connecting with them on such an intimate topic and process. It's its own vibe and energy. Even more, I love seeing what it did to me and the personal growth I have experienced.

I became stronger and more confident. Self-love and self-care became rituals and practices. I faced my biggest enemy (myself) by surviving a trial of where I had to be brutally, BRUTALLY honest. I accepted the no's and failures in life, learned from them and moved on. I've met wonderful people along the way who were genuinely interested in helping, mentoring and listening to my billions and billions of ideas. They kept me grounded, challenged, inspired and realistic. The best and most unexpected part of what entrepreneurship did for me was restoring my childlike spirit and Wild Wild West imagination.

Although there was and will be hardships and disappointments along the way, I am freer than ever! I count my blessings and indulge in the joy and peace from within. I'm truly thrilled for who I am today, the people in my life and where I am going. I have become my own biggest fan and have no problem saying, "Wow, I am extremely proud of myself!"

To all my entrepreneur friends out there, don't forget to be you! Don't forget to choose and include yourself throughout the beginning, middle and end. The business will be there, and the customers will come and go. And, yes, a source of income/profit is crucial to keeping your business alive; it's undeniable. These components are imperative to starting, running, managing and growing a business.

However, as you invest in your business, invest in yourself. Take care of yourself and don't be afraid to treat yourself once in a while. You deserve it! Be your own biggest fan. I really mean every word of it! I see too many people not do this and they ended up feeling lost, burnt out and everything bad. Your business will begin to suffer from across the borders when you are not present, and that's the last thing anyone of us will want. I've been there, done that and still encounter it. You are the most important factor to the whole equation, so own it!

Before you shot gun bringing your idea to life and legally registering it as a business, slow your yee-haw excitement butt down. I'm guilty of this. Haha. Lessons learned. When I'm ecstatic about something, my inner child manifests in full force, and it's hard stopping her. She has already launched off like toddlers do when they're not supposed to have something in their mouths.

To slow yourself down, start by creating a checklist and possibly a list of questions or things you don't know or think you may need to know. Organize your thoughts, ideas and expectations. The beginning phase is crucial, so develop a plan of action and include all the technical and tedious *stuff* before you register your business. This include, but is not limited to, defining your mission, vision, objectives, goals, brand and targeted audience. Look into your competition and the marketplace. Is there a need for what you will be offering? Is there value in your expertise, product, services and/or programs? You will also need to have some working knowledge of your state laws. Will you need to apply for a sales tax permit? What are the safety code violations? What resources are available for business owners? Basically, do your homework.

These last two piece of advices that I will leave you with are two of my favorite things to talk about. It is 1.) Building a support system and 2.) Branding and understanding what that looks like for you as an individual and as a business. I, along with some of the entrepreneurs I have met and befriended, will agree that it can be a lonely path. No one really told me that. Unless you have the resources to hire people right off the bat or is in a partnership of some sort, you will end up taking on several roles at first, which can lead to isolation and depression.

My family and friends are near and dear to me, but most of them do not understand the experiences, processes and emotions of being an entrepreneur and business owner, and that's perfectly fine. You must learn to accept this. I am most fortunate to have my cousin be a part of my support system. She is an entrepreneur and has started two businesses, by herself, while in her twenties. We would meet up for coffee or food and share our lives as solopreneurs.

She is an amazing person and the first person I turn to when I need a second opinion or someone to talk to. Check out her social media at Freelance Artistry and Fave Macarons.

In the age of social media and technology, I started to join Facebook groups geared at entrepreneurs and business owners, networking and mentorship. Although I am an ambivert, I lean more on the introvert side of things when it comes to socializing. For my introverts, this is a great way to start with networking and meeting like-minded people. Back in my days, I had to physically put myself out there and network the good old-fashioned way. I reached out to people, attended functions, workshops, events, introduced myself, or knew someone who knew someone. Networking did wonders for me.

I also set up job shadowing and informational interviews and met with people who were successfully doing what I was interested in. They provided their insights, expertise and time for FREE. You bet I made sure I was the best sponge alive and soaked up as much as possible. After each meeting, I would follow up with an email or thank you card. I found my mentor in these ways. Today, my support group is solid, and I've surrounded myself with people of similar mindsets, attitudes and interests. I protect my energy and steer far from negativity.

This goes hand in hand with "branding"—that super, duper fancy word to sum up who you are, what you're all about and how you are remembered. Before I started my business, I was more focused on finding out who I was and defining what that means. Being Hmong, I was raised on the value of one's reputation and word. My parents' reputation can affect how the community and elders view me and vice versa. I applied this value and aimed to be mindful, intentional and honest in what I say and do. Initially, my main objective was to become well-rounded and respectable.

I started examining my weaknesses, strengths, thoughts, values, morals, etc. and began to pay close attention to what people had to say about me, comparing it to what I thought of myself. In doing so, I began to understand myself through my own eyes and the eyes of others. What comes to people's minds when they hear my name? How do I want them to remember me? What will I choose to accept, reject or change? Ask yourself those questions. Were you able to answer them? My journey started with accepting growth as an ongoing process that requires a level of

Simply Being Mee

engagement and humility. I had to learn to be ok with making mistakes and asking for help.

When I reached the point where I was confident enough to declare who I am, others started trusting and expecting me to be exactly that. My personal brand was born. Branding for my business was a no brainer. I was asking the same questions but now in business lingo versus personal development. Think of brands like Nike and McDonalds. Now, think of their logos and slogans. That is a part of branding. You do not want to rush this part when starting up your business. In fact, I strongly advise you to spend extra time on branding.

If I was to ask you right now to tell me about your business, how successful will you be in doing that? Am I hearing crickets, or will it be a lion's roar? How would you start and what are the things you will say right off the back? Why did you even start? Why not a 9-5 job with security and benefits? What inspired you? What do you offer? Your work culture and atmosphere? Why should I, or any potential clients, choose you? How you talk about your business is another aspect of branding.

Do you need to know exactly what your brand is all about when you first start up? Not necessarily, but you should have a general idea of your business and brand. It's not abnormal if the business and brand take on several transformations throughout its lifetime. Perfection is an ideology. Rebranding is a thing. There are different methods for a business to grow and, with that, there will always be room for improvements. Be open to changes. But, if you don't have the slightest clue about your business and brand, your customers will have an even harder time. With that, tell me your story. I'm all ears.